Nothing Important

Allegorical poems in the pursuit of meaning

A collection of poems from 2017 to 2019

ALEX K. BISHOP

 FriesenPress

Suite 300 - 990 Fort St
Victoria, BC, V8V 3K2
Canada

www.friesenpress.com

Copyright © 2020 by Alex K. Bishop
First Edition — 2020

All rights reserved.

ISBN
978-1-5255-7950-9 (Hardcover)
978-1-5255-7951-6 (Paperback)
978-1-5255-7952-3 (eBook)

1. POETRY, SUBJECTS & THEMES

Distributed to the trade by The Ingram Book Company

Cynicism was born when art and comedy became tools for wealth and distraction rather than a source of happiness.
Happiness then died because nothing was meaningful anymore . . .
So when nothing is meaningful or important,
how can we ever be happy again?

Introduction

Through the three years of writing this book, I've struggled a lot with finding happiness and meaning in some sort of way. My own battles with mental illness also made this a challenge for me, especially now, in my most formative years, as I am just trying to achieve my goals and succeed in some way. I've struggled a lot with expressing my own emotions, and it just so happens that poetry was a medium that I enjoyed the most. The dawning dread of my own existence also pushes me towards a selfish goal: to not be forgotten. We all know that one day we will pass, but living on through our art is **eternal**.

This collection of poems is divided into six essential aspects of meaning: Nature, Love, Religion, Life, Society, and Art. Meaning in nature (or nature's beauty) refers to our relationship with what is natural and how depression creates apathy for the world around you. Meaning in love, and the experience of heartbreak, refers to the intimate relationship with another and the subsequent (yet essential) pain that occurs with separation. Meaning in religion (more specifically, moral conviction) refers to the solidification of personal morals and the rejection of pure moral relativism and moral apathy. Meaning in life refers to our relationship with death and the entire lifetime, along with our relationship with future generations. Meaning in society is the relationship with the people in our community, what we owe each other, and the inevitable shortcomings. Lastly, meaning in art is the birthplace of meaning and subsequently the rebirth of meaning in our relationship with artistic **expression**.

Contents

Part One: Nature

Little Alex's Secret

High above, in the fortress he loves dear,
Evergreen trees keep this sanctuary whole.
Secrets he keeps are of no concern or cause of fear;
Directing your attention to the beauty takes its toll.
Eyeing his gaze to what's unimportant completes him,
Peeping even a small porting of beauty accomplishes this:
Receiving transmissions of gusts flow the harmonic hymn;
Even the clouds provide him with present-time bliss.
Some search seasons, soul searching so saddened;
Still, they could never see the world so simple and shallow,
Ease of mind, in the calm world of his so maddened.
Damned mind, he feels nothing. He is unfortunately hollow.

(Acrostic)

The Traveller

A woman has sought to travel the globe,
A desire of will from the frontal lobe.
She searches far and wide for happiness,
And to overcome her shyness.
She found many little places she feels home,
Secret blissful areas where feet are in loam.
The people with faces are always there jubilant.
The animals of places are never equidistant.
All of them will stay in her mind for days afar.
She is suddenly hit by a car.

In a Willow, in a Tree

In a willow,
In a tree,
A bird I know,
Is what I want to see.

A sign of life,
To my unrest,
But nevermore fife,
I will protest.

If I see a nest,
What would I do?
Do I feel it a pest?
Or their home is there, true?

I think not
What hate has in mind,
But I find fraught
The bird I can't find.

The bird I know
Is no longer here.
With fallen snow,
Due west is unnear.

Cuba

In daylight rays
The beaches of Cuba lays
And the way of waves flow
From darkness below.

The ocean thought romantic,
But this, a stupid antic.
To us, what we feel
As something that's real.

A cool breeze is serene,
But doesn't need abstracts unseen.
Thus the clouds of blue deep sky
Are allowed to be spry.

The clouds, like cattle,
Heave the sky without brattle,
To light the sky on fire,
Then chard night soothed by lyre.

From the beach of Cuba,
There was no light of Luna.
There was only the darkest horizon
From that ocean under; it's a siren.

This great void flatland
Is empty for the sight at hand.
But even in the chard night sealings,
I can't help but find feelings.

Like Drowning

A message received,
Blue and green is ambience perceived.
Such pressure in water is omnipresent,
But I somehow find this pleasant.

Floating so surreal in the dark drink,
I wonder if I'll ever see the sea pink?
Air in the deep dark is a rarity,
But my vision has such clarity.

The fact that I will drown doesn't cause me despair,
When the oppressive force was in fact air!
The abrasive sun's hue refracts
In the presence of this bath it contacts.

Such rays have no power in light,
When the depth of water is too affright.
In letting go our last breath,
I rapidly sink to this deep down depth.

Like my fetus stage, I am nurtured well,
Yet your cold surrounding has a knell.
This knell itself has no sound waves,
Like drowning, waves drown out octaves.

You surround me so invasively,
But the silence coerces so persuasively.
My hair ever seems to sway in your clout,
And my clothes, now dyed green, are stout.

Once white, sea water is now the pigment,
Yet this all seems a figment.
Such sea creatures swarm my presence,
Shining their scales bright blue like lunar *crescence.*

And in this lunar bask, so bestial,
They move to reveal a marine celestial.
Such a giant to this vast sea of creatures,
Your omnipresence is that of emperor features.

Even to mine own self, I am but a krill.
What must I do in good will?
Opening its mouth, such a mighty boom;
It was a roar for respect, not doom.

Clearly the sight of sunken ships
And old bones shows their eclipse.
I do not contest; I open arms,
So that I may flatter its royal charms.

In my thoughts, they spoke to me,
Such a being, I am unworthy to see.
"What Child of dirt has come back,
Come to haunt my palace in the black?"

"Great monarch, pardon my intrusion,
My time with you is but an allusion."
"My Child, you mustn't feel so ill at ease;
We will all become one with the sand and ocean breeze."

With that being said, the creature couldn't stand.
It crumbled from stone and then to sand.
In its last breath, the bubble swallowed me up,
Carrying me to the surface in a buildup.

The expulsion crashed with a bang in the air,
Where a passing boat fished me out so unfair.

The Katsura Tree Haikus

The Katsura tree
Standing tall next to the pond
Memories planted.

The bottom water
Preserves leaves like photographs
Every season.

The commodities
A symbol of our power
Left here in the pond.

Rotten as it is
Leaves, boulders, and geese feces
All a part of one.

Spirit of the pond
Here for many centuries
Tainted by our filth.

For this disrespect
Spirits show what we must pay
The consequences.

Now that we have paid
The pond gives new memories
The Katsura tree.

Frozen Frost

Blue skies are the moonlit nights
That fill the air with frost.
This, an invasion of the senses,
Nevermore a creation of the mind.

The existence fill my presence,
Heightened by my forest journey.
Along these thin-skinned trees,
They do not bother me in my mood.

With light comes direction on the path.
Light has become undone in sight.
But in this frosted roam into the woods,
I cannot help but feel in sanctuary.

For this night, I find my purpose suspended,
Like a private time for fulfilment.
Yet purpose does the same with time.
What use do I find so special tonight?

Pointed questions bring me nowhere;
To where I now roam through the frosted woods,
To find answers to questions I never asked.
Gifts are wasted if they weren't desired.

Hark the crow in its void,
Guiding my chilled, pale skin.
Echo the dimensions you've travelled, friend.
Cold winter winds chill the bones of the dead.

But not this glacier skin I have become.
A raw warmth keeps my flesh whole,
Keeps my night whole.
These eastern winds bring forth wrath.

No matter the cold hatred endured.
These winds beckon faded spirits.
To quench a flame in a heart of old,
I am cold.

The Man, a Bench in the Park

There's a man on a bench,
A park bench, sturdy and firm.
The park is a place of natural stench,
But nothing matters, he will affirm.

From the bench, the man sees the lake.
He sees the shimmer, the shine, the swaying trees.
He says: "All of this was a grand mistake."
He even fails to feel the breeze.

The ducks quack,
The birds chirp,
The fish *bloop*.
He knows cold, like coal-black flak.
He knows that anyone can usurp.
He knows a lower ground that most can't stoop.

He knows
The lows.

The water will flow
Along into the river,
But the man can't follow
His way himself, not even a sliver.

He closes his eyes
To feel the sun shine on his face.
One of his days will know highs
And hope it leaves without apace.

But the wind gusts the leaves.
The leaves have no say
In who leaves and who will stay.
We might as well be nature's sheaves.

Unlike the great question "why,"
He lets out a sigh.

Fade

This Eden of mine
Is a living place so divine.
Those memories so fond
Give this place a special bond.

Those days in the Spring are over,
Where winter decays moreover.
To walk through this garden,
Beckons tears to harden.

To see this lively and jubilant place,
Now rotten and decrepit, is a disgrace.
The funky flowers and groovy grass
Are either decayed or overgrown in mass.

To experience this new form grotesque
Would freeze me so statuesque.
To become like the statues surrounded
Would surely end this story expounded.

To hear the silence so haunted
Kills the spirit daunted.
The animals that lived so spry
Abandoned the home they would occupy.

Peer through the mist to reveal the heart,
Now but a cyst as its counterpart.
It pumps, beats, and bleeds a slushy pus
All over the snow-covered yard in a muss.

The niveous blanket is omnipotent,
Exciting my hatred for the precipitant.
Come forth, murderer from above!
Nothing else matters hereof.

You, my garden vast,
Were meant to be my crutch to a time passed.
What has corrupted your sanctity?
Whatever happened to your crudity?

But the leafless trees are still standing
Despite the needs they are demanding.
The pond, although putrid and awry,
Will always be full and never dry.

Despite all that you've become
And all that I'll overcome,
I'll always think of you highly today,
If you promise not to fade away.

Part Two: Love

My Darling

Looking up at the cold night's black abyss,
Such wonder is fond of bliss!
This is where the silver-white pearl sits!
What an enticing glow it emits.

So close, I could pluck you from the sky.
But you only show each month, being so shy.
I will wait regardless, only for you to strike my mind.
But the wall that we must face will brace through time to be unkind.

Looking down at the deep empty space,
Your radiant glow is still presenting your grace.
Such a tempting sight for wolves and poets to adore,
But drowning depths and great pressures I do not ignore.

So what will I do in my salty mood?
I hate this joke you present so crude:
My darling pearl, you beckon my find,
But the wall that we must face will brace through time to be unkind.

I digress, venturing into this abyssal space weather,
Because death will brace through time so that we could be together.

The Fountain

You cry too softly darling, try harder.
Like the cold stone faces of the fountain sides.
If only your eyes could see this stone ardour,
Maybe you'd see how ironic this coincides.

Your black heart still beats, even after the highlight.
But my blue fountain hides your worst quality.
Hollow bones and mellow stones, without twilight.
My love for you died, and from death birthed prodigality.

Who knew it would be so easy? To build such beauty
Took a lot out of yourself, just to be whole.
I suppose you'll only be my secret duty
From which you're still buried in that forsaken hole.

Who knew that such envious perfection, so lovely,
Could be so, so, deadly.

Sitting on a Bus

Simply stated, I'm stranded on a bus.
Travelling fast, I don't make a fuss.
Such a blur, the passing buildings and houses,
Like dull dust, I never think of the husbands and spouses.

Sometimes I see somewhere very grand,
Maybe a church, a hospital, or the forests of fairyland.
I pass the gardens now, the lovely park's lost.
I would've loved to see the colours and not exhaust

The moment with a flash to the construction near.
Once passed, I see more art and colour on the clear,
Lit buildings around the city that I can't stop to see.
Perhaps this was meant to be.

Perhaps living is seldom.
Perhaps I will become my grandmother in beldam.
But I reconsider, stopping at a green light.
At the bus stop, a woman, travelling this time of night.

It was a moment frozen in time.
I didn't care, I didn't even bother to rhyme.
I snap from my hypnotism.
She doesn't get on the bus, despite optimism.

It matters little when the bus leaves without me.
I think I'll walk, despite air so frosty.

A Ghost for You, Fine Muse

Oh, darling, fine muse.
Cold, lonely winter is not news.
But the presence, a vision
That left your sight is not superstition.

The overwhelming presence
Of the shadow of non-misfeasance
Looms in the trees near
Your window light blear.

I, a phantom in thought,
You may imagine me naught.
But to my new-found plight,
I cry, I wail in the night.

In your bed, while you sleep,
The wisping wraith enters in a creep.
Whenever the wind you feel,
In the night appears, I am real.

Look into my spirit eyes
And you'll see who I am likewise.
I've watched you change,
Exchange and rearrange.

Let me touch your wings of thrall
And watch the feathers fall.
When you awake, I am gone,
For I am beyond human sight drawn.

Through the window, I glide,
When this ghost has died.
It may chill you
To feel me come back new.

But a specter haunts surreal
And in the night, I am real.

Fantasy and More

Would it seem strange
To last a love without change?
All things must end, to much dismay,
But imbalance is this outweigh.

I know this is the end
Because much time we expend.
Hold me, dear, closely;
The wick of the candle loosely

Resembles the fuse burning too quickly,
That will end us both slickly.
Does it all finish without escape?
Or does it just change shape?

I'll meet your eyes
And see the darkness incise.
The candle smoulders soon
To an unlikely tune.

"La Vie en rose,"—Edith Piaf.
How fitting on her behalf.
The omnipresent embrace is sudden,
But embraces matter not sullen.

Because it's you for me
And for me is thee.
And once I notice you moved on,
Thus I sense in me gone.

My heart that beats.

Love Will Find You

No matter what you do,
Love will find you.
You may feel it a threat,
But this you will regret.

Whether it's the moon,
Looking down like a mother rune.
Weather it's the breeze,
An invasive force with mild please.

No matter when the day,
Love will show the way.
You may fall along the path;
Rely on support, you nailed the lath.

Fur of a feral dog is still soft,
We change like the fur so oft.
Fir forests are evergreen so lush,
We are eternal thoughts like pine brush.

No matter who you see,
Love will leave you be.
You may find some heartbreak,
But that's what love will take.

Missed those who you longed,
Hoping they'd stay prolonged.
Mist those solid foundations,
And bear the force of love's creations.

A Sailor's Grief

By lord, these salty bones pain me.
Weighing me down, cracking my back.
I'll still go to the shores on days rainy
Just to see the ocean's long track.

Oh by, I still feel the force of her pushing.
Down by the rocky beach, I'm swaying,
'Cause my fluthered self's been rushing
To sail again instead of staying.

Just being at the beach reminds the mind.
Swaying the same way I did on the ship.
She didn't deserve a fate so unkind.
The ropes had too much of a tight grip;

I'll sit down here to light me pipe.
Curse these winds for blowing the flame!
Every match I light is gone with gripe.
As if the ocean points the finger of blame.

It's been a while since I've met the ocean,
Like a lover you once knew regretfully.
Fourteen calendars wasted to time's endless motion,
While I sit here in anger so fretfully.

The changing skies urge the prod.
I walk knee-high into the drink,
And curse ye the taking god,
While I throw me old pipe in the damned sink.

The night sky shows a true wrath
Enjoying their prize sitting beneath.
I shake my fist to the brewing storm in the bath,
Shouting more *feckin* words through my teeth.

I'll lay my heavy arse on the rocks,
And rest my head for just a moment.
The patrollers came from the docks
To see if my lifeless body was dead by foment.

"A ship is a sailor's soul
But the first mate is the sailor's heart."
I lost both, tethered to the mast poll.
I held her hand until we were apart.

Hearing the flask empty into my mouth
Calls back the flooding hull.
We charted out, west by south,
Only ten kilometers out from the harbour Schull.

I'll replace the old bucket, never the best friend.
The nights of wonder are what I'll save.
I can hear the crackling storm I will fend,
Mixed with the crackling rocks of the receding wave.

Bloody Kisses

Is there painless love?
The youth is always thought sweet.
As time request my behove,
So does the love of pain we meet.

It's fascinating our time aside,
When we shared bloody kisses.
Yet an ocean always has a changing tide.
It's this current that love misses.

Can someone force love like they do pain?
Or is it merely the sum?
"Nothing more romantic than rain,"
I'd say in the cold, so numb.

Even the most pleasant memory can strike,
Because we know it didn't last.
I know what it feels like,
To stand there while the moment passed.

The youth is always thought sweet.
How couldn't it be?
There was never deceit.
The loving pain is both for you and me.

Remember the Time

Remember thee
And remember me.
For long since past
The time gone so fast.

Although I cause mither,
The pain is your wither.
When a mass of time spent
Now return not a single cent.

I'll lay down the tracks,
So that I may fill in the cracks.
For a friend so dear,
Live not in fear.

Hope is now our joy,
That we may build back our tabloid.
A collection tainted
Can now be repainted.

Ramen & Sushi

A meal well made,
Well worth what was paid,
Is the dinner date I'll eat,
While I converse with the person I'm here to meet.

Sushi wrapped in eel,
And ramen tasting so surreal.
Both are devoured so vicious,
It was quite delicious.

After eating, our date wasn't over yet,
Because there wasn't much for us to fret.
The night was a fresh fruit,
And there was more for us in pursuit.

Laughing

When do you laugh?
When do you cry?
If you feel torn in half,
Is your laugh really at me in eye?

Laugh like a child,
Or laugh like a madman.
You were there when I smiled
To wipe it away before it began.

If you take all the joy,
Will it sustain you?
Your laughing is a ploy.
Did you know that you knew?

And All That Could Have Been

Forgotten songs that I'll sing to your thought,
For all the effort I wrought.
To the battles that we would lose or win,
And all that could have been.

Hope is the carrot on an optimistic stick
And the drive, a thorn on our heel to prick.
But the prize was twin souls from within;
And all that could have been.

I would have seen those daylight rays of the morning
If it all played out in the beautiful adorning.
I could see the future so rich without this chagrin;
And all that would have been.

Don't believe in the perfection of two minds alike.
Some don't have the best form of psych.
We both know the nightmares beneath our skin,
And all that would have been.

I wanted us to be greater than the falling rain.
I'm not sure if any of that will remain.
We deserved the stars in our palms herein,
And all that should have been.

But if we alone can't be enough to grow,
Where can we go?
For the reasons we end and not to begin,
And all that should have been.

Ill Met by Moonlight

It is bad luck we met when moonlight's shining,
But us, chanceful, desire the crisp blue lining.
We meet our lustrous moonly eyes;
The trance is like witchcraft or a wiccan guise.

Such a blue aura fits our night serene.
Making love is our prayer to Selene.
Fit for ourselves, we'll never see day's sight,
So we pursue each other to chase the moonlight.

Speak to me the words I'll write,
Enchant the way we forever see the night.
As it should forever be,
The darkest nights are a deep green we'll never see.

Bloom her insightful blue aura, magical Hecate,
And thus baffle the idea of doomed fate.
Together we found fires of the chard night simmering,
Under the stars and the moonlight shimmering.

Part Three: Religion

The Serpent's Egg

I throw myself through the open doors of intimacy without hesitation.
I suppose I'll crawl sluggishly towards the place of my eternal duration.
In life, my malice only served to benefit those who enjoyed my
salty frustration.
And all those foods and drinks of masses leave me in starvation.
What I have left is mine and only mine, even though I face
divine taxation.
I have done nothing wrong, harmed no one, and created art, so there's
certainly time for adoration
Before I charge with hellish fury into the place of boiling blood and
my damnation.

Limbo

The Spirits of a life
That knew those most strife,
Can be found in their keep;
Limbo, the land of sighs and weep.

Ask them, if you may,
Ask them if they remember the light of day.
"Yes, now I'm reminded how much it's missed."
"No, I have no memories of value that exist."

What wisdom lurks in these creatures?
An eternity to talk and learn from teachers
Brings only self-fulfilment, no greater cause;
Leaving behind their human flaws.

Haunting shadows cloud everything,
You have merely visited the first ring.
Come now, sweet Dante, deeper we must go.
To ascend above, we must so below.

Lust

The Spirits of a life
That pursue the flesh rife,
Can be found in this motion;
Lust, a gust of endless locomotion.

Talking is futile.
Restless fluidity can be brutal.
Having known no rest,
Forever awake in their arrest.

Is this punishment right for the act?
Having no rest for physical attracts?
Such a natural state of mind
Is neverending, always inclined.

Such gusting wind can give a sting,
Yet you've visited only the second ring.
Come now, sweet Dante, deeper we must go.
To ascend above, we must so below.

Gluttony

The Spirits of gloom,
That knew only to consume,
Are wallowed deep in this pit;
Gluttony, a urinal of shit.

Belly down, they cannot stand
The putrid smell of this fecal land.
For knowing not moderation,
They sluggishly endure their endless duration.

How fitting must this be,
To bask in the carelessness they couldn't see.
This humility seems quite cruel
For overflowing hungers for fuel.

Such a horrid view of a bodily spring.
Welcome to the third ring.
Come now, sweet Dante, deeper we must go.
To ascend above, we must so below.

Greed

The Spirits of riches
Who scratched the wealthy itches,
Can be found under weights.
Their guilt is what the wealthy awaits.

For wealth hoarded or lavishly spent,
Large bags of guilt are what to represent.
To push this weight forever in a battle so un-thrilling,
Like Sisyphus, is the neverending billing.

What of those most charitable?
Are these used for their moral label?
What of their inheritance after death,
When this charity brings no comfort to the dying breath?

Heavy the head that bears the crown of a king.
Halfway through, this is the fourth ring.
Come now, sweet Dante, deeper we must go.
To ascend above, we must so below.

Wrath

The Spirits of angry fire,
That know a hatred desire,
Can be found under Styx's water;
Wrath, a river of endless slaughter.

Phlegyas guides the travelling brother,
While the hateful fight each other
And those gloomy and moody folk
Simply gurgle beneath the water they soak.

Although I do believe those *fightful*
Belong here so rightful.
Why punish those who aren't jolly?
Why is a lack of joy an innocent one's folly?

Anger has no fulfilment to bring.
Pass through the fifth ring.
Come now, sweet Dante, deeper we must go.
To ascend above, we must so below.

Heresy

The Spirits of their dissension,
Who thought not of the convention,
Are kept in a state quite horrific;
Heresy, tombs for those most prolific.

These people are sent to their dooms
To be burned forever in flaming tombs.
The tombs are open, yet it's not freedom it shows.
In the end of days, those tombs close.

No apostasy, no schisms,
Only those major deviants of other isms,
Satanism, Atheism, Darwinism, etcetera.
The list includes a plethora.

Deviant thoughts are clutched in a cling.
You've finally seen the sixth ring.
Come now, sweet Dante, deeper we must go.
To ascend above, we must so below.

Violence

The Spirits of a life,
That knew the power of a knife,
Are divided from one to three.
Violence, a river of blood and forest of trees.

The outer ring, murderers drown in blood boiling.
The inner ring, blasphemers in a flaming desert broiling.
The middle, however, suicides turn into trees
To be fed on my Harpies.

I admit this place is fitting,
For violence against others and themselves unwitting.
Those woe now grow into trees and bushes rooted,
Where perhaps their soul will return their body suited.

Do not walk in the shadow of the harpies' wing.
Only two more down past the seventh ring.
Come now, sweet Dante, deeper we must go.
To ascend above, we must so below.

Fraudulence

The Spirits of inception,
Masters of deception,
Are found lost in the Malebolge vast;
Fraudulence, for those deceivers of the past.

Ride down on the Geryon beast,
The representation of the phoniest,
To see the ten bolgias at their base.
Fitting for each type of fraud in their place.

Oh, so fitting, every one of those ditches,
Like the reversed heads for the sorcerers and witches,
Or the flatterers immersed in excretions,
And the thieves bitten by serpents with flaming secretions.

Pass those people most fake.
Nowhere left but Cocytus, the frozen lake.
Come now, sweet Dante, deeper we must go.
To ascend above, we must so below.

Treachery

The Spirits of betrayal,
Who will meet their defrayal,
Are found in the deepest of pits;
Treachery, the Cocytus lake where Lucifer sits.

Each round of the lake is more severe.
Deeper into the ice, the more guilt sincere.
From bowing necks to shield the frozen wind blowing,
To full submersion in grotesque forms showing.

Caina, murderers of kin.
Antenora, traitors of the state from within.
Ptolomea, betrayers of a trusted guest.
Judecca, snakes against a lord blest.

Let Satan's wings continue to freeze in leaven,
While Dante and Virgil continue to Heaven.
Some don't deserve their price bestow,
But the rest deserve the worst below.

Rusted Moon

I try to look up at the nightlight,
But my eyes blister without its white.
The moon is withered and rusted.
Left to rot in its state so distrusted.

But the fiery colour still glows,
Like a wrathful eye that now arose.
Staring intently in the minds of woe.
Staring intensely in the mind I know.

Such a haunting sight it shows,
Not quite a blood moon, yet the worst it chose.
It neither lights my way,
Nor excites mine eyeing dismay.

All I see is judgment away,
Overpowering me in a way.
To finally be confronted by the distant entity,
A bask I entice for my identity.

Part Four: Life

Make Like the Tree You Are

Make like the tree you are,
And speak up! The rustling leaves are faint to the forests' barks of bark.
And grow up! Every plant must run its standard way of living, you may
find bizarre.
And come here! Do you believe that I'm not here to listen? Wrong.
For you I will hark.

And go away. All birds that fall from my nestled branches go on with
their lives elsewhere.

Like the rock you will be,
Your smooth young pulp will grow strong and ruff.
Your very masculine appeal hath also feminine qualities with the
sprouting of children you will see.
Your large and beautiful trunk will have had a life to live and collapse
when you've had enough.

You're going to die for the sake of the seed.

Keep Skipping in Life, Young Lad

As a young child very small, very blank,
They skipped along the river bank.
A little older, a teenager bold and brass,
They decided to leave and skip class.

Much later, an adult bound to clockwork,
They think that today they'll skip work.
They got cold feet, their love was shedding,
So they decided to skip their own wedding.

Old age took him, even in his final breath,
Still, they decided to skip their father's death.
It was soon their time too, an event so crucial,
But there was no skipping their own death, this fiducial.

If you were a holy, you'd believe they were here,
Skipping away, as ghosts do, with a ghostly cheer.

House, Home

A House is a Home,
When the new are born in nursery
Or the dead are kept in catacomb
All of which are ordinary.

All Homes hold secrets unknown,
But a House holds none.
Tucked away neatly or buried under a stone,
Secrets are always seen under the midnight sun.

The Library is for simple knowledge,
But the dining room is where
Our ancient ways are acknowledged.
Yet the coming together is unaware.

But a Home can also be divided,
When the born must leave the nest.
A House divided had only leaders misguided,
Believing they had more power than the rest.

Four walls and roof is all bone,
But the core makes the Home of his
A burning fire of Hearthstone
Because the Home is where the Heart is.

The Rough Stone

This is an ode to you, rough stone,
My presence comes with leaves blown.
You, rough stone, move not to wind;
You have no fret with headwind

When you no longer have a journey.
The grey stone is now green with ferny
Grass and father moss living;
I find it a shame that you're dead forgiven.

You, rough stone, are smaller from erosion.
You, to me, lose more to time like corrosion.
One day, you will not be an image in eyes;
I still have breath, with my children likewise.

But now's the time, rough stone, I leave.
This tombstone, to me, I will not grieve.

Unbreakable Desire to See Tomorrow

Some days are fraught,
Some days are agitating.
But end it, I will not
Because of ice skating.

I do not know suicide
Because of ice cream,
Not because the upside
Has shown light in dream.

Just wait, tomorrow!
Enjoy a pistachio,
Or a fancy chapeau?
Enjoy a cawing crow!

Joy doesn't come from the deep,
It's trivial! Ignorant!
It's neither rich nor cheap,
It's You, perception *invigorant*.

Leave your room,
Go outside!
See those flowers bloom,
And find senses once denied!

Entropy

Ivory madness and dry water,
Lettered words scattered further.
Obituaries are hymns from clocks,
Verbalizing looks like rocks.
Empathy's a rarity,
Yearning brings clarity.
Outside sees nothing inside,
Until I'm set aside.
Dandy darling, Dutch,
Every day's gone from touch.
Acrostic angst isn't delicious,
Rather you eat something vicious.
Ataxia eats headworms slow—
Let it go.
Window widow, glass breaks,
Alive spits in flakes.
Young you–me smells the blue,
Singing softly, Can't Lose You.

The Time of a Maritimer

A father is a man who will pass.
I do, I do miss my father dearly,
Like a strong foundation you surpass,
But the crumble bears a cost severely.

He's gone now, a natural form.
'Tis so unnatural for a father to bury the child.
Nothing can replace a cold love so warm,
And neither the child has humbly smiled.

I'll reflect here at Point Pleasant Park,
From the lookoff where the ocean is in full view.
I see the islands and so patiently hark,
Waiting for that voice I know so true.

I cry not for the passing of my father;
It solves no problems for this young rhymer.
It'll only make it harder;
A tear won't rewind the Time of a Maritimer.

I'll imagine he's there, on the islands far,
Seeing me, and waving along with the ocean waves,
As if the gusting wind fulfils my hark afar,
Screaming from distant island of graves.

All to tell me he's proud.
And forever he'll scream loud.

Ghost Forms

Fleeting forms are leaving,
To let me rest once more.
But while I'm still heaving,
I will not open that door.

"Learn your lesson,"
They tell the unforgiven.
No more pain will it lessen,
For the end of a journey striven.

I'll sit by my bed,
Middle of the night,
And watch the door with dread,
To never let it leave my sight.

A twist of the knob,
And the soft push of force,
Reveals the shadowy blob:
The ghost form's source.

This isn't a demon of hell,
Nor a vile spirit of Aether;
It is a mirror I try to dispel,
My silhouette bonded together.

I stand from my bed
To greet this manifest,
Taking me to where it led,
The place where I rest.

What Ghosts are these,
That no one sees?
Who are those spirit lights yonder,
That have a guilt I ponder?

They know who I am.
They speak of my *quodam*
To reveal a knowledge no one boasts:
I am those ghosts.

The Balance Haikus

I know solitude
I walk down the forest road
Fresh among the trees.

Where we have come from
Life would give us the first breath
Wind among the trees.

Leaves will fall from trees
As they did so the last year
Start of the ending.

Life and Death balanced
More we live, the more we die
Wilted flowers bloom.

Pedals fill the sky
Life will give them back to us
Beauty is fragile.

Where we lay to rest
Death would give us the last breath
Leaves will fill the ground.

Life must always end
This is what gives life purpose
Wind among the trees.

Part Five: Society

Sympathy for the Confined

What is hell?
How do we define this well?
We must search for the human nature
And apply to the razor
That cuts out the essence
And leaves life without pleasance.

They can only move in a chair.
I find this a nightmare.
Immobilized, confined.
It was not hard for me to find.
I could see in this moment
This was hell potent.

Confined to their electric chair,
It seems like such death without health care.
To move freely, freely,
A luxury that I feel for them deeply.
Life had been crippled,
And I feel for them *simpled.*

These are one of us, too,
It seems absurd to exclude their view.
Crippling loneliness,
Now I find hell's lowliness.
In their eyes, I find them,
Sympathy for the confined outcome.

Keep Slipping in Life, Young Lad

Where are you, young lad? When are you?
Those drugs must break reality's hue.
You slip so swiftly out of friendships,
This could be fixed by tightening your grip.

You slip even further, losing family.
Why have you let your kin fall through gravity?
You slip past them all, society shuns.
Now you'll only end alone in the slums.

You slip through the cracks of your integrity.
Who are you, young lad? You've lost self-familiarity.
You slip with a crack as you lose your mind.
Confusion is your reason's wheeze you blind.

You slip with nothing to fall on beneath.
The breaking down of reality has no bequeath.

The Burden of Happiness

Oh, what unnatural feeling,
Others must only be happy.
But what seems more revealing,
The coldness seems snappy.

How must I only find joy?
Is it through the empty wallet?
Is the happy man the consumer's cloy?
Western Capitalism is what they call it.

"The simple superficial leaning"—
A very masculine emotion.
Our days of no more meaning;
But to what end is this notion?

The natural feeling of sorrow;
Oh, what a feeling when flows.
It's merely a mood we aim to borrow.
To value a mood will make it go.

To Plato, it was virtue all along;
Wisdom, Courage, Moderation, and Justice.
To balance these is happiness strong,
Because the struggle is just us.

No more food for my hunger,
No more water for my thirst,
No more madness of the monger;
I quench my happiness first.

I'll Bury You in the Spring

The Spring is our time together,
But you left me without peace.
This dreadful storm has explosive weather,
Having you leave me without one piece.

Such an oppressive silence, my reproach,
Then the sound of an overwhelming siren.
Like Sirens, they call on me to approach,
To make a fitting end, like those of Lord Byron.

But their smoky breath devours hope,
So that I may become another statistic.
If you were here, my child, I would elope;
Instead I'll watch these rebels become fascistic.

Why do we smile and laugh when at the same beats,
Blood runs violently in the streets?
The Horror. The horror so surreal.
Who wants to see us suffer or beg to their heel?

Through the dust, the orphaned child nearby,
The child looks too eager to die.
As if god will take them and finally feed them,
Only after they endure the mayhem.

Please don't cry, child, you'll waste water.
It's hard to say you remind me of my daughter.
Like her before you, I will say the same thing:
I will bury you in the Spring.

Night Crawlers

Walking at night can be frightening on its own,
The dismay heightened by what's unknown.
Stop your pacing down the line;
Hear the silence of the streets you cannot define.
A gust of wind down that darkened alley,
Brings no comfort to your finale.
You gaze intensely without fear,
Looking around for dangers unclear.
Swiftly leaving your tracks behind,
You feel proud for facing nothing but your mind.
To your mistake, they simply watched with please.
They were in the trees.

The Light

Look away from its radiance!
Its sight is a maddening omniscience.
Do not fret your new-found plight.
Do not look at the green light.

You cannot know why it is so,
Just keep your head down low.
Have faith in my instruction,
Or it will be your abduction.

The Autumn air, so cold,
Is a comforting touch untold.
But with your absence it would be too much
For this old heart to bear a frozen touch.

I plead you to follow my way.
Tell your eyes to stay away.
Whether or not you think I'm wrong or right,
Do not look at the green light.

Part Six: Art

The Aesthetical Murder

With such strength, his sword is carried,
Ready to strike, at a moment varied.
He spots the foe, pleasantly unconcerned,
With the drawing of his blade, the other turned.

Unwilling to die, he flees so heartedly,
Not out of fear, but love guardedly.
But no matter the speed, the sword will strike.
His pounce leads fire and fury, so much dreamlike.

The peak is a pose, so glorious in art,
You would not suppose a murder will take part.
The decent is not defeat, aiming precise and stiff.
The swinging sword marks a powerful whiff,

And thus such a clean cut is made moonlit.
The instant slash makes the skin split.
No blood at first,
But then the warm lava immersed.

The legs kept moving, but the head stayed.
The look on his face still seemed afraid.
The man with the sword is an artist with ruction,
He is not concerned with creation, only destruction.

In the pool of blood, the promise was made,
A promise to make the creation of life delayed.
From dirt, the body lays in marinade,
To be decomposed and then decayed.

Or maybe a young lad will find him bloody,
And finish the work by making him muddy.
Buried deep, a secret he will keep.
Maybe a lie, a peep, where words will seep.

No concern for the man with a sword,
Because in the act, he finds his reward.

Ode to Calliope

Calliope, muse of epics!
An ode short, unlike narratives
That you inspire for the heroes.
And heroines, likewise you love,
To seek and desire freedom
In the reams of inspiration.
Adventurous your thoughts must be,
Racing around land like Hermes,
Trying to find those in your need
For an adventure so epic.
'Tis the life so grand for exploit,
None question if this, your desire.

Ode to Clio

To you, Clio, History muse!
Like Cleopatra, age is yours.
The ages recorded are yours.
The events so crucial are yours.
All yours, when none to remember
These events and time in their eyes.
Set in stone, your words are the truth
Of who we were and who we'll be.
But historians may not know,
If you give caution or prospect.
Most times, society needs you
To give our future ambition.

Ode to Erato

Oh, Erato, muse of fierce love!
Love is an emotion of yours.
Love is what you define for them,
So that we may join together.
Sexual desires seem fitting
For your basic needs satisfied,
But love is more in divine eyes.
Selflessness true is what you give
To men and women in their hope
Of finding emotions so good.
So keep their thoughts excited hot
To find a pleasure that cuts deep.

Ode to Polyhymnia

Polyhymnia, muse of hymns!
A religious voice most can hear,
Think you quarrel with Erato
Over the desires of people:
A sister free but sinful, too.
But you love her for expressions
When you bring what is the humble
Thoughts of godly wisdom in play.
Desires are not inspiration,
When the hymns chant something much more
Than the mortal need for what's real,
When a hymn can make them believe.

Ode to Melpomene

Melpomene, muse of those woes!
A sweet kiss you bring the mournful,
When certain doom strikes in their lives.
Though you don't cause them suffering,
You are there for those in your need
To vent emotions into art
So that they may find Thalia.
Jealousy, you shouldn't notice
Because to inspire will save them
From a cruel fate such as sadness
Or a nightmare for your wishes:
"The perpetual tragedy."

Ode to Thalia

Oh, Thalia, joy-making muse!
Art in theatre makes the drama.
Although cathartic you may be,
A life of sorrow is not primed
From the human condition kind.
Comedy you inspire often
Gives them hope and optimism
In Melpomene's tragedy.
Both necessary complements
That love each other's endeavour.
Dear doctor, give the medicine
Of laughter so sweet and tender.

Ode to Urania

Urania, muse of the stars!
The great infinity above
Is a plane that's ripe to inspire.
How could one treat the nebula
With such care in describing them?
You may try your best to invoke
Subliminal Astronomy,
But those cosmonauts high in space
Can truly experience this.
Even then, looking back to earth
Invokes other inspiration:
A love for home amongst the stars.

Ode to Terpsichore

Terpsichore, the dancing muse!
The art of you is body moves.
It is an expression wordless.
No paint from the artists brushes,
No song from singers music.
The body is the tool dancers
Use to display your divine thoughts.
Sometimes the dance so orderly
Is balanced with dance chaotic.
The joy of dance is natural,
With emotions turned physical.
Your dance burns rhythmic emotion.

Ode to Euterpe

Oh, Euterpe, songwriting muse,
Inspiring me in all these odes!
A song for them, your sisters dear.
Song has become strong in culture,
When words and rhythms are thorough
In conveying timely zeitgeists.
But nevermore will the voice die
When forevermore you inspire.
Your beauty is the soft, peaceful
Pitch of a voice that lullabies
And excites the audiences.
Never end endless divine song!

Bless Your Body Art

Aesthetics.
Odd to word them,
Because they're meant to be felt.
Like felt, the fabric,
The fabric of beauty
Was felt that moment.
Inked words and inked art.
Sat at the bench on the boardwalk,
Filtering down the view.
A catch through the fog lenses, I find.
Sunglasses filter out great radiance,
Like this sunlit day.
Naturally, they'd want to filter your radiance.
But I caught wind
And gazed my attention.
Naturally lit skin revealed its fullness.
Such acute senses struck by art.
It's an ignorant feeling,
Yet the sublime has been met.
Most art is met on canvas, walls, or ceilings,
But our days have found a new mode.
The Hennas and Tattoos glow.
Art is a mystery.
The light refracting off the water
Made the tattoos dance.
Like the butterflies that flew,
Scattering around the rosemary branch.

Or the faces of the lost loved ones,
Who seem so animated and alive.
What kind of sorcery is this?
Have they been cursed by Ancients?
Or have they been blessed by far away Saints?
Do these questions matter?
The evening mist grew along the harbour.
Like a great colossus,
The foggy hand waved through us
And turned the sky a deep orange.
In the ambient light,
Such emotion was ripe to seize.
I approach the shape of inked beauty
Like how I would approach art in a museum.
With such a smooth voice, I confess to them:
"Bless your body art."
This is the Aesthetics worded.

Nothing Important

Are you afraid?
Afraid of meaning's death?
What more can we gain?
Anything.

Are you afraid?
Afraid to die?
Where will we go, since meaning died?
Nowhere.

Are you afraid?
Afraid to live without hope?
Do we hold anything sacred anymore?
Nothing important.

Are you afraid?
Afraid of the future?
What's worth living after meaning?
Created meaning.

Are you afraid?
Afraid of this absurdity?
How can we ever be happy again?
Sincere earnestness.

Are you afraid?
Afraid of empty truth?
Is there any escape from ourselves?
There shouldn't be.

Are you afraid?
Afraid of yourself?
Are we dreading the rebirth of meaning?
Not anymore.

Are you afraid?
Afraid to be happy?
Are you happy?

CPSIA information can be obtained
at www.ICGtesting.com
Printed in the USA
LVHW091635251020
669765LV00026B/1199